Spiritual Notebook

# GAYATRI MANTRA

Aum Bhur Bhuvah Svah
Tatsaviturvarenyam
Bhargo Devasyadhimahi
Dhiyo Yo Nah Prachodayat

Aum Bhur Bhuvah Svah, Tatsaviturvarenyam
Bhargo Devasyadhimahi, Dhiyo Yo Nah Prachodayat

_____

_____

_____

_____

_____

_____

_____

_____

_____

We meditate on the glory of that Being who has
produced this universe; may He enlighten our minds

Aum Bhur Bhuvah Svah, Tatsaviturvarenyam
Bhargo Devasyadhimahi, Dhiyo Yo Nah Prachodayat

_____

_____

_____

_____

_____

_____

_____

_____

_____

We meditate on the glory of that Being who has
produced this universe; may He enlighten our minds

Aum Bhur Bhuvah Svah, Tatsaviturvarenyam
Bhargo Devasyadhimahi, Dhiyo Yo Nah Prachodayat

_____

_____

_____

_____

_____

_____

_____

_____

We meditate on the glory of that Being who has
produced this universe; may He enlighten our minds

Aum Bhur Bhuvah Svah, Tatsaviturvarenyam
Bhargo Devasyadhimahi, Dhiyo Yo Nah Prachodayat

---

---

---

---

---

---

---

---

---

We meditate on the glory of that Being who has
produced this universe; may He enlighten our minds

Aum Bhur Bhuvah Svah, Tatsaviturvarenyam
Bhargo Devasyadhimahi, Dhiyo Yo Nah Prachodayat

---

---

---

---

---

---

---

---

---

We meditate on the glory of that Being who has
produced this universe; may He enlighten our minds

Aum Bhur Bhuvah Svah, Tatsaviturvarenyam
Bhargo Devasyadhimahi, Dhiyo Yo Nah Prachodayat

---

---

---

---

---

---

---

---

---

We meditate on the glory of that Being who has
produced this universe; may He enlighten our minds

Aum Bhur Bhuvah Svah, Tatsaviturvarenyam
Bhargo Devasyadhimahi, Dhiyo Yo Nah Prachodayat

_____

_____

_____

_____

_____

_____

_____

_____

_____

We meditate on the glory of that Being who has
produced this universe; may He enlighten our minds

Aum Bhur Bhuvah Svah, Tatsaviturvarenyam
Bhargo Devasyadhimahi, Dhiyo Yo Nah Prachodayat

_____

_____

_____

_____

_____

_____

_____

_____

_____

We meditate on the glory of that Being who has
produced this universe; may He enlighten our minds

Aum Bhur Bhuvah Svah, Tatsaviturvarenyam
Bhargo Devasyadhimahi, Dhiyo Yo Nah Prachodayat

_____

_____

_____

_____

_____

_____

_____

_____

_____

We meditate on the glory of that Being who has
produced this universe; may He enlighten our minds

Aum Bhur Bhuvah Svah, Tatsaviturvarenyam
Bhargo Devasyadhimahi, Dhiyo Yo Nah Prachodayat

_____

_____

_____

_____

_____

_____

_____

_____

_____

_____

We meditate on the glory of that Being who has
produced this universe; may He enlighten our minds

Aum Bhur Bhuvah Svah, Tatsaviturvarenyam
Bhargo Devasyadhimahi, Dhiyo Yo Nah Prachodayat

---

---

---

---

---

---

---

---

---

We meditate on the glory of that Being who has
produced this universe; may He enlighten our minds

Aum Bhur Bhuvah Svah, Tatsaviturvarenyam
Bhargo Devasyadhimahi, Dhiyo Yo Nah Prachodayat

---

---

---

---

---

---

---

---

---

We meditate on the glory of that Being who has
produced this universe; may He enlighten our minds

Aum Bhur Bhuvah Svah, Tatsaviturvarenyam
Bhargo Devasyadhimahi, Dhiyo Yo Nah Prachodayat

---

---

---

---

---

---

---

---

We meditate on the glory of that Being who has
produced this universe; may He enlighten our minds

Aum Bhur Bhuvah Svah, Tatsaviturvarenyam
Bhargo Devasyadhimahi, Dhiyo Yo Nah Prachodayat

_____

_____

_____

_____

_____

_____

_____

_____

_____

We meditate on the glory of that Being who has
produced this universe; may He enlighten our minds

Aum Bhur Bhuvah Svah, Tatsaviturvarenyam
Bhargo Devasyadhimahi, Dhiyo Yo Nah Prachodayat

_____

_____

_____

_____

_____

_____

_____

_____

_____

We meditate on the glory of that Being who has
produced this universe; may He enlighten our minds

Aum Bhur Bhuvah Svah, Tatsaviturvarenyam
Bhargo Devasyadhimahi, Dhiyo Yo Nah Prachodayat

_____

_____

_____

_____

_____

_____

_____

_____

_____

We meditate on the glory of that Being who has
produced this universe; may He enlighten our minds

Aum Bhur Bhuvah Svah, Tatsaviturvarenyam
Bhargo Devasyadhimahi, Dhiyo Yo Nah Prachodayat

_____

_____

_____

_____

_____

_____

_____

_____

_____

We meditate on the glory of that Being who has
produced this universe; may He enlighten our minds

Aum Bhur Bhuvah Svah, Tatsaviturvarenyam
Bhargo Devasyadhimahi, Dhiyo Yo Nah Prachodayat

---

---

---

---

---

---

---

---

---

We meditate on the glory of that Being who has
produced this universe; may He enlighten our minds

Aum Bhur Bhuvah Svah, Tatsaviturvarenyam
Bhargo Devasyadhimahi, Dhiyo Yo Nah Prachodayat

_____

_____

_____

_____

_____

_____

_____

_____

_____

We meditate on the glory of that Being who has
produced this universe; may He enlighten our minds

Aum Bhur Bhuvah Svah, Tatsaviturvarenyam
Bhargo Devasyadhimahi, Dhiyo Yo Nah Prachodayat

_____

_____

_____

_____

_____

_____

_____

_____

We meditate on the glory of that Being who has
produced this universe; may He enlighten our minds

Aum Bhur Bhuvah Svah, Tatsaviturvarenyam
Bhargo Devasyadhimahi, Dhiyo Yo Nah Prachodayat

---

---

---

---

---

---

---

---

We meditate on the glory of that Being who has
produced this universe; may He enlighten our minds

Aum Bhur Bhuvah Svah, Tatsaviturvarenyam
Bhargo Devasyadhimahi, Dhiyo Yo Nah Prachodayat

---

---

---

---

---

---

---

---

---

We meditate on the glory of that Being who has
produced this universe; may He enlighten our minds

Aum Bhur Bhuvah Svah, Tatsaviturvarenyam
Bhargo Devasyadhimahi, Dhiyo Yo Nah Prachodayat

_____

_____

_____

_____

_____

_____

_____

_____

We meditate on the glory of that Being who has
produced this universe; may He enlighten our minds

Aum Bhur Bhuvah Svah, Tatsaviturvarenyam
Bhargo Devasyadhimahi, Dhiyo Yo Nah Prachodayat

_____

_____

_____

_____

_____

_____

_____

_____

_____

We meditate on the glory of that Being who has
produced this universe; may He enlighten our minds

Aum Bhur Bhuvah Svah, Tatsaviturvarenyam
Bhargo Devasyadhimahi, Dhiyo Yo Nah Prachodayat

_____

_____

_____

_____

_____

_____

_____

_____

_____

We meditate on the glory of that Being who has
produced this universe; may He enlighten our minds

Aum Bhur Bhuvah Svah, Tatsaviturvarenyam
Bhargo Devasyadhimahi, Dhiyo Yo Nah Prachodayat

_____

_____

_____

_____

_____

_____

_____

_____

_____

We meditate on the glory of that Being who has
produced this universe; may He enlighten our minds

Aum Bhur Bhuvah Svah, Tatsaviturvarenyam
Bhargo Devasyadhimahi, Dhiyo Yo Nah Prachodayat

---

---

---

---

---

---

---

---

---

We meditate on the glory of that Being who has
produced this universe; may He enlighten our minds

Aum Bhur Bhuvah Svah, Tatsaviturvarenyam
Bhargo Devasyadhimahi, Dhiyo Yo Nah Prachodayat

_____

_____

_____

_____

_____

_____

_____

_____

_____

We meditate on the glory of that Being who has
produced this universe; may He enlighten our minds

Aum Bhur Bhuvah Svah, Tatsaviturvarenyam
Bhargo Devasyadhimahi, Dhiyo Yo Nah Prachodayat

_____

_____

_____

_____

_____

_____

_____

_____

_____

We meditate on the glory of that Being who has
produced this universe; may He enlighten our minds

Aum Bhur Bhuvah Svah, Tatsaviturvarenyam
Bhargo Devasyadhimahi, Dhiyo Yo Nah Prachodayat

---

---

---

---

---

---

---

---

---

We meditate on the glory of that Being who has
produced this universe; may He enlighten our minds

Aum Bhur Bhuvah Svah, Tatsaviturvarenyam
Bhargo Devasyadhimahi, Dhiyo Yo Nah Prachodayat

_____

_____

_____

_____

_____

_____

_____

_____

_____

We meditate on the glory of that Being who has
produced this universe; may He enlighten our minds

Aum Bhur Bhuvah Svah, Tatsaviturvarenyam
Bhargo Devasyadhimahi, Dhiyo Yo Nah Prachodayat

_____

_____

_____

_____

_____

_____

_____

_____

_____

_____

We meditate on the glory of that Being who has
produced this universe; may He enlighten our minds

Aum Bhur Bhuvah Svah, Tatsaviturvarenyam
Bhargo Devasyadhimahi, Dhiyo Yo Nah Prachodayat

_____

_____

_____

_____

_____

_____

_____

_____

_____

We meditate on the glory of that Being who has
produced this universe; may He enlighten our minds

Aum Bhur Bhuvah Svah, Tatsaviturvarenyam
Bhargo Devasyadhimahi, Dhiyo Yo Nah Prachodayat

_____

_____

_____

_____

_____

_____

_____

_____

_____

We meditate on the glory of that Being who has
produced this universe; may He enlighten our minds

Aum Bhur Bhuvah Svah, Tatsaviturvarenyam
Bhargo Devasyadhimahi, Dhiyo Yo Nah Prachodayat

_____

_____

_____

_____

_____

_____

_____

_____

We meditate on the glory of that Being who has
produced this universe; may He enlighten our minds

Aum Bhur Bhuvah Svah, Tatsaviturvarenyam
Bhargo Devasyadhimahi, Dhiyo Yo Nah Prachodayat

---

---

---

---

---

---

---

---

---

We meditate on the glory of that Being who has
produced this universe; may He enlighten our minds

Aum Bhur Bhuvah Svah, Tatsaviturvarenyam
Bhargo Devasyadhimahi, Dhiyo Yo Nah Prachodayat

---

---

---

---

---

---

---

---

---

We meditate on the glory of that Being who has
produced this universe; may He enlighten our minds

Aum Bhur Bhuvah Svah, Tatsaviturvarenyam
Bhargo Devasyadhimahi, Dhiyo Yo Nah Prachodayat

_____

_____

_____

_____

_____

_____

_____

_____

_____

We meditate on the glory of that Being who has
produced this universe; may He enlighten our minds

Aum Bhur Bhuvah Svah, Tatsaviturvarenyam
Bhargo Devasyadhimahi, Dhiyo Yo Nah Prachodayat

---

---

---

---

---

---

---

---

---

We meditate on the glory of that Being who has
produced this universe; may He enlighten our minds

Aum Bhur Bhuvah Svah, Tatsaviturvarenyam
Bhargo Devasyadhimahi, Dhiyo Yo Nah Prachodayat

_____

_____

_____

_____

_____

_____

_____

_____

_____

We meditate on the glory of that Being who has
produced this universe; may He enlighten our minds

Aum Bhur Bhuvah Svah, Tatsaviturvarenyam
Bhargo Devasyadhimahi, Dhiyo Yo Nah Prachodayat

_____

_____

_____

_____

_____

_____

_____

_____

_____

We meditate on the glory of that Being who has
produced this universe; may He enlighten our minds

Aum Bhur Bhuvah Svah, Tatsaviturvarenyam
Bhargo Devasyadhimahi, Dhiyo Yo Nah Prachodayat

_____

_____

_____

_____

_____

_____

_____

_____

_____

We meditate on the glory of that Being who has
produced this universe; may He enlighten our minds

Aum Bhur Bhuvah Svah, Tatsaviturvarenyam
Bhargo Devasyadhimahi, Dhiyo Yo Nah Prachodayat

_____

_____

_____

_____

_____

_____

_____

_____

_____

We meditate on the glory of that Being who has
produced this universe; may He enlighten our minds

Aum Bhur Bhuvah Svah, Tatsaviturvarenyam
Bhargo Devasyadhimahi, Dhiyo Yo Nah Prachodayat

---

---

---

---

---

---

---

---

---

We meditate on the glory of that Being who has
produced this universe; may He enlighten our minds

Aum Bhur Bhuvah Svah, Tatsaviturvarenyam
Bhargo Devasyadhimahi, Dhiyo Yo Nah Prachodayat

_____

_____

_____

_____

_____

_____

_____

_____

_____

We meditate on the glory of that Being who has
produced this universe; may He enlighten our minds

Aum Bhur Bhuvah Svah, Tatsaviturvarenyam
Bhargo Devasyadhimahi, Dhiyo Yo Nah Prachodayat

_____

_____

_____

_____

_____

_____

_____

_____

_____

We meditate on the glory of that Being who has
produced this universe; may He enlighten our minds

Aum Bhur Bhuvah Svah, Tatsaviturvarenyam
Bhargo Devasyadhimahi, Dhiyo Yo Nah Prachodayat

_____

_____

_____

_____

_____

_____

_____

_____

_____

We meditate on the glory of that Being who has
produced this universe; may He enlighten our minds

Aum Bhur Bhuvah Svah, Tatsaviturvarenyam
Bhargo Devasyadhimahi, Dhiyo Yo Nah Prachodayat

_____

_____

_____

_____

_____

_____

_____

_____

_____

We meditate on the glory of that Being who has
produced this universe; may He enlighten our minds

Aum Bhur Bhuvah Svah, Tatsaviturvarenyam
Bhargo Devasyadhimahi, Dhiyo Yo Nah Prachodayat

_____

_____

_____

_____

_____

_____

_____

_____

_____

We meditate on the glory of that Being who has
produced this universe; may He enlighten our minds

Aum Bhur Bhuvah Svah, Tatsaviturvarenyam
Bhargo Devasyadhimahi, Dhiyo Yo Nah Prachodayat

_____

_____

_____

_____

_____

_____

_____

_____

We meditate on the glory of that Being who has
produced this universe; may He enlighten our minds

Aum Bhur Bhuvah Svah, Tatsaviturvarenyam
Bhargo Devasyadhimahi, Dhiyo Yo Nah Prachodayat

_____

_____

_____

_____

_____

_____

_____

_____

_____

We meditate on the glory of that Being who has
produced this universe; may He enlighten our minds

Aum Bhur Bhuvah Svah, Tatsaviturvarenyam
Bhargo Devasyadhimahi, Dhiyo Yo Nah Prachodayat

---

---

---

---

---

---

---

---

---

We meditate on the glory of that Being who has
produced this universe; may He enlighten our minds

Aum Bhur Bhuvah Svah, Tatsaviturvarenyam
Bhargo Devasyadhimahi, Dhiyo Yo Nah Prachodayat

---

---

---

---

---

---

---

---

---

We meditate on the glory of that Being who has
produced this universe; may He enlighten our minds

Aum Bhur Bhuvah Svah, Tatsaviturvarenyam
Bhargo Devasyadhimahi, Dhiyo Yo Nah Prachodayat

_____

_____

_____

_____

_____

_____

_____

_____

_____

We meditate on the glory of that Being who has
produced this universe; may He enlighten our minds

Aum Bhur Bhuvah Svah, Tatsaviturvarenyam
Bhargo Devasyadhimahi, Dhiyo Yo Nah Prachodayat

_____

_____

_____

_____

_____

_____

_____

_____

_____

We meditate on the glory of that Being who has
produced this universe; may He enlighten our minds

Aum Bhur Bhuvah Svah, Tatsaviturvarenyam
Bhargo Devasyadhimahi, Dhiyo Yo Nah Prachodayat

_____

_____

_____

_____

_____

_____

_____

_____

_____

_____

We meditate on the glory of that Being who has
produced this universe; may He enlighten our minds

Aum Bhur Bhuvah Svah, Tatsaviturvarenyam
Bhargo Devasyadhimahi, Dhiyo Yo Nah Prachodayat

_____

_____

_____

_____

_____

_____

_____

_____

_____

We meditate on the glory of that Being who has
produced this universe; may He enlighten our minds

Aum Bhur Bhuvah Svah, Tatsaviturvarenyam
Bhargo Devasyadhimahi, Dhiyo Yo Nah Prachodayat

---

---

---

---

---

---

---

---

---

We meditate on the glory of that Being who has
produced this universe; may He enlighten our minds

Aum Bhur Bhuvah Svah, Tatsaviturvarenyam
Bhargo Devasyadhimahi, Dhiyo Yo Nah Prachodayat

_____

_____

_____

_____

_____

_____

_____

_____

We meditate on the glory of that Being who has
produced this universe; may He enlighten our minds

Aum Bhur Bhuvah Svah, Tatsaviturvarenyam
Bhargo Devasyadhimahi, Dhiyo Yo Nah Prachodayat

_____

_____

_____

_____

_____

_____

_____

_____

_____

We meditate on the glory of that Being who has
produced this universe; may He enlighten our minds

Aum Bhur Bhuvah Svah, Tatsaviturvarenyam
Bhargo Devasyadhimahi, Dhiyo Yo Nah Prachodayat

———————————————————————

———————————————————————

———————————————————————

———————————————————————

———————————————————————

———————————————————————

———————————————————————

———————————————————————

We meditate on the glory of that Being who has
produced this universe; may He enlighten our minds

Aum Bhur Bhuvah Svah, Tatsaviturvarenyam
Bhargo Devasyadhimahi, Dhiyo Yo Nah Prachodayat

_____

_____

_____

_____

_____

_____

_____

_____

_____

_____

We meditate on the glory of that Being who has
produced this universe; may He enlighten our minds

Aum Bhur Bhuvah Svah, Tatsaviturvarenyam
Bhargo Devasyadhimahi, Dhiyo Yo Nah Prachodayat

---

---

---

---

---

---

---

---

We meditate on the glory of that Being who has
produced this universe; may He enlighten our minds

Aum Bhur Bhuvah Svah, Tatsaviturvarenyam
Bhargo Devasyadhimahi, Dhiyo Yo Nah Prachodayat

_____

_____

_____

_____

_____

_____

_____

_____

_____

_____

We meditate on the glory of that Being who has
produced this universe; may He enlighten our minds

Aum Bhur Bhuvah Svah, Tatsaviturvarenyam
Bhargo Devasyadhimahi, Dhiyo Yo Nah Prachodayat

_____

_____

_____

_____

_____

_____

_____

_____

We meditate on the glory of that Being who has
produced this universe; may He enlighten our minds

Aum Bhur Bhuvah Svah, Tatsaviturvarenyam
Bhargo Devasyadhimahi, Dhiyo Yo Nah Prachodayat

_____

_____

_____

_____

_____

_____

_____

_____

_____

We meditate on the glory of that Being who has
produced this universe; may He enlighten our minds

Aum Bhur Bhuvah Svah, Tatsaviturvarenyam
Bhargo Devasyadhimahi, Dhiyo Yo Nah Prachodayat

_____

_____

_____

_____

_____

_____

_____

_____

_____

We meditate on the glory of that Being who has
produced this universe; may He enlighten our minds

Aum Bhur Bhuvah Svah, Tatsaviturvarenyam
Bhargo Devasyadhimahi, Dhiyo Yo Nah Prachodayat

_____

_____

_____

_____

_____

_____

_____

_____

_____

_____

We meditate on the glory of that Being who has
produced this universe; may He enlighten our minds

Aum Bhur Bhuvah Svah, Tatsaviturvarenyam
Bhargo Devasyadhimahi, Dhiyo Yo Nah Prachodayat

_____

_____

_____

_____

_____

_____

_____

_____

_____

We meditate on the glory of that Being who has
produced this universe; may He enlighten our minds

Aum Bhur Bhuvah Svah, Tatsaviturvarenyam
Bhargo Devasyadhimahi, Dhiyo Yo Nah Prachodayat

_____

_____

_____

_____

_____

_____

_____

_____

_____

_____

We meditate on the glory of that Being who has
produced this universe; may He enlighten our minds

Aum Bhur Bhuvah Svah, Tatsaviturvarenyam
Bhargo Devasyadhimahi, Dhiyo Yo Nah Prachodayat

_____

_____

_____

_____

_____

_____

_____

_____

_____

We meditate on the glory of that Being who has
produced this universe; may He enlighten our minds

Aum Bhur Bhuvah Svah, Tatsaviturvarenyam
Bhargo Devasyadhimahi, Dhiyo Yo Nah Prachodayat

_____

_____

_____

_____

_____

_____

_____

_____

_____

_____

We meditate on the glory of that Being who has
produced this universe; may He enlighten our minds

Aum Bhur Bhuvah Svah, Tatsaviturvarenyam
Bhargo Devasyadhimahi, Dhiyo Yo Nah Prachodayat

---

---

---

---

---

---

---

---

---

We meditate on the glory of that Being who has
produced this universe; may He enlighten our minds

Aum Bhur Bhuvah Svah, Tatsaviturvarenyam
Bhargo Devasyadhimahi, Dhiyo Yo Nah Prachodayat

_____

_____

_____

_____

_____

_____

_____

_____

_____

We meditate on the glory of that Being who has
produced this universe; may He enlighten our minds

Aum Bhur Bhuvah Svah, Tatsaviturvarenyam
Bhargo Devasyadhimahi, Dhiyo Yo Nah Prachodayat

_____

_____

_____

_____

_____

_____

_____

_____

_____

We meditate on the glory of that Being who has
produced this universe; may He enlighten our minds

Aum Bhur Bhuvah Svah, Tatsaviturvarenyam
Bhargo Devasyadhimahi, Dhiyo Yo Nah Prachodayat

_____

_____

_____

_____

_____

_____

_____

_____

_____

We meditate on the glory of that Being who has
produced this universe; may He enlighten our minds

Aum Bhur Bhuvah Svah, Tatsaviturvarenyam
Bhargo Devasyadhimahi, Dhiyo Yo Nah Prachodayat

---

---

---

---

---

---

---

---

We meditate on the glory of that Being who has
produced this universe; may He enlighten our minds

Aum Bhur Bhuvah Svah, Tatsaviturvarenyam
Bhargo Devasyadhimahi, Dhiyo Yo Nah Prachodayat

_____

_____

_____

_____

_____

_____

_____

_____

_____

We meditate on the glory of that Being who has
produced this universe; may He enlighten our minds

Aum Bhur Bhuvah Svah, Tatsaviturvarenyam
Bhargo Devasyadhimahi, Dhiyo Yo Nah Prachodayat

_____

_____

_____

_____

_____

_____

_____

_____

_____

We meditate on the glory of that Being who has
produced this universe; may He enlighten our minds

Aum Bhur Bhuvah Svah, Tatsaviturvarenyam
Bhargo Devasyadhimahi, Dhiyo Yo Nah Prachodayat

---

---

---

---

---

---

---

---

---

We meditate on the glory of that Being who has
produced this universe; may He enlighten our minds

Aum Bhur Bhuvah Svah, Tatsaviturvarenyam
Bhargo Devasyadhimahi, Dhiyo Yo Nah Prachodayat

_____

_____

_____

_____

_____

_____

_____

_____

_____

We meditate on the glory of that Being who has
produced this universe; may He enlighten our minds

Aum Bhur Bhuvah Svah, Tatsaviturvarenyam
Bhargo Devasyadhimahi, Dhiyo Yo Nah Prachodayat

_____

_____

_____

_____

_____

_____

_____

_____

_____

_____

We meditate on the glory of that Being who has
produced this universe; may He enlighten our minds

Aum Bhur Bhuvah Svah, Tatsaviturvarenyam
Bhargo Devasyadhimahi, Dhiyo Yo Nah Prachodayat

---

---

---

---

---

---

---

---

We meditate on the glory of that Being who has
produced this universe; may He enlighten our minds

Aum Bhur Bhuvah Svah, Tatsaviturvarenyam
Bhargo Devasyadhimahi, Dhiyo Yo Nah Prachodayat

---

---

---

---

---

---

---

---

---

We meditate on the glory of that Being who has
produced this universe; may He enlighten our minds

Aum Bhur Bhuvah Svah, Tatsaviturvarenyam
Bhargo Devasyadhimahi, Dhiyo Yo Nah Prachodayat

_____

_____

_____

_____

_____

_____

_____

_____

_____

We meditate on the glory of that Being who has
produced this universe; may He enlighten our minds

Aum Bhur Bhuvah Svah, Tatsaviturvarenyam
Bhargo Devasyadhimahi, Dhiyo Yo Nah Prachodayat

_____

_____

_____

_____

_____

_____

_____

_____

_____

_____

We meditate on the glory of that Being who has
produced this universe; may He enlighten our minds

Aum Bhur Bhuvah Svah, Tatsaviturvarenyam
Bhargo Devasyadhimahi, Dhiyo Yo Nah Prachodayat

_____

_____

_____

_____

_____

_____

_____

_____

We meditate on the glory of that Being who has
produced this universe; may He enlighten our minds

Aum Bhur Bhuvah Svah, Tatsaviturvarenyam
Bhargo Devasyadhimahi, Dhiyo Yo Nah Prachodayat

---

---

---

---

---

---

---

---

---

We meditate on the glory of that Being who has
produced this universe; may He enlighten our minds

Aum Bhur Bhuvah Svah, Tatsaviturvarenyam
Bhargo Devasyadhimahi, Dhiyo Yo Nah Prachodayat

_____

_____

_____

_____

_____

_____

_____

_____

_____

We meditate on the glory of that Being who has
produced this universe; may He enlighten our minds

Aum Bhur Bhuvah Svah, Tatsaviturvarenyam
Bhargo Devasyadhimahi, Dhiyo Yo Nah Prachodayat

_____

_____

_____

_____

_____

_____

_____

_____

_____

We meditate on the glory of that Being who has
produced this universe; may He enlighten our minds

Aum Bhur Bhuvah Svah, Tatsaviturvarenyam
Bhargo Devasyadhimahi, Dhiyo Yo Nah Prachodayat

---

---

---

---

---

---

---

---

---

We meditate on the glory of that Being who has
produced this universe; may He enlighten our minds

Aum Bhur Bhuvah Svah, Tatsaviturvarenyam
Bhargo Devasyadhimahi, Dhiyo Yo Nah Prachodayat

_____

_____

_____

_____

_____

_____

_____

_____

_____

_____

We meditate on the glory of that Being who has
produced this universe; may He enlighten our minds

Aum Bhur Bhuvah Svah, Tatsaviturvarenyam
Bhargo Devasyadhimahi, Dhiyo Yo Nah Prachodayat

_____

_____

_____

_____

_____

_____

_____

_____

_____

We meditate on the glory of that Being who has
produced this universe; may He enlighten our minds

Aum Bhur Bhuvah Svah, Tatsaviturvarenyam
Bhargo Devasyadhimahi, Dhiyo Yo Nah Prachodayat

_____

_____

_____

_____

_____

_____

_____

_____

_____

We meditate on the glory of that Being who has
produced this universe; may He enlighten our minds

Aum Bhur Bhuvah Svah, Tatsaviturvarenyam
Bhargo Devasyadhimahi, Dhiyo Yo Nah Prachodayat

_____

_____

_____

_____

_____

_____

_____

_____

_____

We meditate on the glory of that Being who has
produced this universe; may He enlighten our minds

Aum Bhur Bhuvah Svah, Tatsaviturvarenyam
Bhargo Devasyadhimahi, Dhiyo Yo Nah Prachodayat

_____

_____

_____

_____

_____

_____

_____

_____

_____

We meditate on the glory of that Being who has
produced this universe; may He enlighten our minds

Aum Bhur Bhuvah Svah, Tatsaviturvarenyam
Bhargo Devasyadhimahi, Dhiyo Yo Nah Prachodayat

_____

_____

_____

_____

_____

_____

_____

_____

_____

We meditate on the glory of that Being who has
produced this universe; may He enlighten our minds

Aum Bhur Bhuvah Svah, Tatsaviturvarenyam
Bhargo Devasyadhimahi, Dhiyo Yo Nah Prachodayat

_____

_____

_____

_____

_____

_____

_____

_____

_____

We meditate on the glory of that Being who has
produced this universe; may He enlighten our minds

Aum Bhur Bhuvah Svah, Tatsaviturvarenyam
Bhargo Devasyadhimahi, Dhiyo Yo Nah Prachodayat

_____

_____

_____

_____

_____

_____

_____

_____

_____

We meditate on the glory of that Being who has
produced this universe; may He enlighten our minds

Aum Bhur Bhuvah Svah, Tatsaviturvarenyam
Bhargo Devasyadhimahi, Dhiyo Yo Nah Prachodayat

---

---

---

---

---

---

---

---

---

We meditate on the glory of that Being who has
produced this universe; may He enlighten our minds

Printed in Great Britain
by Amazon

27347570R00057